# William Shakespeare

## Stewart Ross

This edition published in 2008 by
Evans Brothers Ltd.
2A Portman Mansions
Chiltern Street
London W1U 6NR

British Library Cataloguing in Publication Data

Ross, Stewart
    William Shakespeare. - Rev. ed. - (Writers and their times)
    1. Shakespeare, William, 1564-1616 - Biography - Juvenile
    literature 2. Dramatists, English - Early modern, 1500-1700
    - Biography - Juvenile literature
    I. Title
    822.3'3

ISBN: 9780237535872

Printed in Dubai

## Acknowledgements

Consultant – Dr Catherine Alexander, The Shakespeare Birthplace Trust

Editor – Su Swallow
Designer – Ann Samuel
Production – Jenny Mulvanny
Picture Research – Victoria Brooker

For permission to reproduce copyright material, the author and publishers gratefully acknowledge the following:

Cover: (top) Private Collection Bridgeman Art Library (bottom left) From the RSC Collection with the permission of the Governors of the Royal Shakespeare Theatre (bottom centre) Corbis/Everett (bottom right) Robert Harding Picture Library pages 3: (top) Philip Mould, Historical Portraits Ltd, London/Bridgeman Art Library page 5 Mary Evans Picture Library page 6 Walker Art Gallery, Liverpool/Bridgeman Art Library. Board of Trustees: National Museums & Galleries on Merseyside page 7 (top) Mary Evans Picture Library (bottom) National Maritime Museum, London/Bridgeman Art Library page 8 (top) Andrew Ward/Life File (bottom) Mary Evans Picture Library page 9 (top) Philip Mould, Historical Portraits Ltd, London/Bridgeman Art Library (bottom) Mary Evans Picture Library page 10 Guildhall Library, Corporation of London/Bridgeman Art Library page 11 (top) Private Collection, Bridgeman Art Library (bottom) Private Collection/Bridgeman Art Library page 12 (top) Mary Evans Picture Library (bottom) Mary Evans Picture Library page 13 Mary Evans Picture Library page 14 (top) Mary Evans Picture Library (bottom) British Library/Bridgeman Art Library page 15 (top) Robert Harding Picture Library (middle) Roy Miles Gallery, 29 Bruton Street, London W1/Bridgeman Art Library page 16 (top) Mary Evans Picture Library (bottom) Private Collection/Bridgeman Art Library page 17 (top) Richard Kalina/Shakespeare's Globe (bottom) Adina Tovy/Robert Harding Picture Library page 18 (left) Mary Evans Picture Library (right) Bolton Museum and Art Gallery, Lancashire/Bridgeman Art Library page 19 The Shakespeare Centre Library, Stratford-upon-Avon/RSC's Richard III, 1984 page 20 (top) The Shakespeare Centre Library, Straford-upon-Avon (bottom) Private Collection/Bridgeman Art Library page 21 (top) Yale Centre for British Art, Paul Mellon Collection/Bridgeman Art Library (bottom) The Shakespeare Centre Library, Stratford-upon-Avon/RSC's Macbeth, 1986 page 22 The Shakespeare Centre Library, Stratford-upon-Avon/RSC's Macbeth, 1986 page 23 (top) The Shakespeare Centre Library, Stratford-upon-Avon/RSC's Macbeth, 1988 (bottom) The Shakespeare Centre Library, Stratford-upon-Avon/RSC's Othello, 1989 page 24 (top) The Shakespeare Centre Library, Stratford-upon-Avon/RSC's The Merchant of Venice, 1987 (bottom) Stapleton Collection/Bridgeman Art Library page 25 (top) York City Art Gallery/Bridgeman Art Library (bottom) Stratford Church, Stratford-upon-Avon/Bridgeman Art Library page 26 Corbis/Everett page 27 Robbie Jack Photography

# William Shakespeare

# Contents

# Shakespeare's England

**The intelligent and charismatic Queen Elizabeth I (1558-1603), guiding star of the Elizabethan Age.**

William Shakespeare was born in the small market town of Stratford-upon-Avon in April 1564. Elizabeth I, the Virgin Queen, was in the sixth year of her reign. She ruled over some three million people in England and Wales. In theory she ruled Ireland, too, but the troubled island was largely beyond her control. Scotland, under Elizabeth's cousin Mary Queen of Scots, was a separate country. It was unusual for England and Scotland to be ruled by queens, for women were thought inferior to men. The law did not even allow them to own property by themselves. Elizabeth died childless in 1603 and her crown passed to Mary's son James. He was then king of both Scotland and England (James VI and I).

## A monarch's power

A monarch was not just a symbol. The king or queen was personally responsible for government. Elizabeth and James called parliaments to help pass new laws or raise money, but important day-to-day business remained in their own hands and those of their chosen ministers. The court, usually based in one of the royal palaces, was the key power base in the land.

### The state of monarchy

Elizabeth did not believe in setting out the powers of a monarch in too much detail. Her successor, King James, had no such worries. He told parliament in 1610:

> 66 *The state of monarchy is the supremest thing upon earth. For kings are not only God's lieutenants upon earth, and sit upon God's throne, but even by God himself they are called gods.* 99

## Rich and poor

London was by far the biggest city in the kingdom. In 1600 only three other English towns (Norwich, Bristol and York) had populations over 10,000. The great majority of people lived in the country and made a living from agriculture.

Everyone belonged to a definite social class, decided by their birth and wealth. In theory, it was possible to tell someone's class by the clothes they wore. Until King James' time it was actually illegal for a poor person to dress like a wealthy lady or gentleman! At the top of

---

## Shakespeare's spelling

Before the first English books were printed in the 1470s, the language varied widely between different parts of the country. Printing helped to settle it down, but even in Shakespeare's time there were no hard and fast rules for spelling and grammar. The playwright himself, for example, spelt his own name several different ways, such as Shakespear, Shakespeare and Shakspear!

**Children playing in the Long Gallery of Knole, Kent. A gallery, up to 30 metres long, was the latest fashion in large country mansions.**

society was a tiny class of titled aristocrats, or nobles, such as Elizabeth's favourite, the Earl of Leicester. Then came a small class of well-off gentlemen. Shakespeare's success enabled him to buy into this class in 1596. Below the gentlemen and their wives came the merchants and skilled workers.

The bulk of the population, however, were poor farmers, labourers or unemployed 'vagrants'. The gap between the top and bottom of society was enormous. The nobility lived in great mansions, dressed in silks and satins and employed dozens of servants. Working class families dwelt in hovels and could never be sure where their next meal would come from.

## Law and order

Violence might flare up at any moment. Henry VII, Elizabeth's grandfather, won his crown on the battlefield. All the Tudor monarchs faced armed rebellion. In 1605 King James only just escaped being blown up in the Gunpowder Plot. There was no police force and no regular army. The Protestant Church of England was vital to hold society together. Everyone had to go to church, where prayers were said for the monarch. Priests taught that rebellion was against the law of God and Man.

**English fireships scatter the Spanish Armada as it lies anchored off Calais, August 1588. The defeat of the Armada made English hearts swell with patriotic pride.**

### This sceptred isle

The authorities were suspicious of Shakespeare's *Richard II* because it was about a king losing his crown. Nevertheless, John of Gaunt's patriotic speech captured the mood of the country:

> *This royal throne of kings, this sceptred isle,*
> *This earth of majesty, this seat of Mars,*
> *This other Eden, demi-paradise,*
> *This fortress built by nature for herself*
> *Against infection and the hand of war,*
> *This happy breed of men ...*
> *This blessèd plot, this earth, this realm, this England ...*

# Stratford-upon-Avon

▲ Shakespeare's birthplace in Henley Street, Stratford-upon-Avon, one of the most popular tourist attractions in the country. (Right) An 18th century print of the house.

**W**illiam was the third child of Mary and John Shakespeare. We do not know the exact date of his birth, but he was baptised on 26 April and had probably been born a few days before.

The Shakespeares lived in a handsome house on Henley Street. It still survives, much altered, and is shown to visitors as William's birthplace. It was also where John Shakespeare worked as a manufacturer of leather goods, such as purses. By today's reckoning Stratford was no more than a village. It was surrounded by open countryside and during his childhood William must have got to know country ways.

## Country life

The countryside in Shakespeare's time was much emptier than today. There were more woods, streams and wild, uncultivated places. There were no railways and the roads were unmade tracks. The speediest travel was on horseback and most journeys were on foot. People thought nothing of walking 30 kilometres a day.

Candles were expensive, so the lives of ordinary people were determined by the rising and setting of the sun. They rose at dawn and went to bed at nightfall, which meant long days in the summer and short, dark ones in the winter. Families generally all slept in the same room. An open fire, also used for cooking, provided warmth. Most clothes and household goods were home-made.

### Here's flowers for you

Shakespeare, like everyone else of his day, knew the names of the trees, flowers and birds he saw all around him. He often used this country knowledge in his plays:

**66** *Perdita: ... Here's flowers for you:*
*Hot lavender, mints, savory, marjoram,*
*The marigold that goes to bed wi' th' sun,*
*And with him rises, weeping; these are flowers*
*Of middle summer ...*

[The Winter's Tale] **99**

## Pounds and pence

A labourer earned about £7 a year, or six (old) pence a day. A day's wages bought a chicken, a mug of beer and three loaves of bread. There was not much left over for luxuries. When he began writing, William was paid about £5 for a play. This was good money, but nothing compared with the £50 that a rich person might spend on a single suit of clothes.

## School and marriage

We know little of William's early life. Because his father was a leading citizen of Stratford, he almost certainly attended the local church and the (boys only) grammar school. The curriculum was based around the study of Latin. English was considered too vulgar to be studied seriously. William's plays are full of references to Latin authors, which probably means he reached a high standard in the language.

The next thing we know for certain is that in November 1582, when William was 18, he married the 26-year-old Anne Hathaway. The following May she gave birth to a daughter, Susanna. Twins, Hamnet and Judith, followed in 1585. William and Anne lived with his parents. We have no idea how he earned a living at this time. In fact, we have no record of him at all until he turned up London in 1592.

### When he killed a calf...

There are many legends of Shakespeare's youth. Some say he was a poacher, others a travelling actor. John Aubrey, born only a few years after Shakespeare's death, said he worked as a schoolmaster. As a boy, Aubrey declares, Shakespeare had

> *... exercised his father's trade, but when he killed a calf he would do it in a high style, and make a speech.*

## Wrong playwright?

Because we know so little about Shakespeare's life, some people think his plays were not written by him at all. A man with Shakespeare's modest education, they argue, could never have written such fine works. So who did? Many names have been put forward, including Christopher Marlowe, Francis Bacon, the Earl of Oxford – and even Queen Elizabeth herself!

**A marble bust of Shakespeare carved about 1741.**

**A romantic painting (1907) of Stratford Grammar School in Shakespeare's time. The young Shakespeare would probably not have been so well turned out!**

# London

Shakespeare was probably in his mid-20s when he first went to London. Arriving in the city must have been one of the most amazing experiences of his life. The capital, with almost 200,000 inhabitants, was about thirteen times bigger than any other city in the country. It was noisier, too, and dirtier, smokier, richer, busier, more dangerous and much more exciting.

## Keep the peace here, Ho!

Violence was common on the London streets. In *Henry IV Part II* Sergeant Fang attempts to arrest the rogue Sir John Falstaff on behalf of Mistress Quickly:

> FANG: *Sir John, I arrest you at the suit of Mistress Quickly.*
> FALSTAFF: *Away, varlets!... Throw the quean in the channel!*
> QUICKLY: *Throw me in the channel? I'll throw thee in the channel! Wilt thou, Wilt thou, thou bastardly rogue? Murder, murder!...*
> FANG: *A rescue a rescue!*
> QUICKLY: *Good people, bring a rescue or two...*
> PAGE: *Away, you scullion!... I'll tickle your catastrophe!*
> CHIEF JUSTICE: *(entering) What is the matter? Keep the peace here, ho!*

## Publique houses

In his *Survey of London* (1598), John Stow noted that beyond Bishopsgate (near where Shakespeare lived in the 1590s), 'north of Finsbury Fields, are builded two publique houses for the acting and shewe of comedies, tragedies, and histories, for recreation. Whereof one is called the Courtein [Curtain], the other the Theatre'.

## Acting is sinful

Puritans, who wanted to 'purify' the Church of England of its Roman Catholic aspects, strongly disapproved of the theatre. Acting was sinful, they argued, because it was pretence. They also hated men dressing as females, and flamboyant costumes.

**London in 1572. Note the single bridge and the open fields close to the City.**

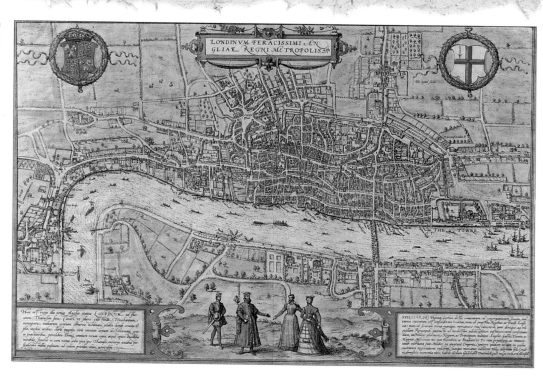

## The growing city

By Shakespeare's time the original walled city on the north bank of the Thames had spread in all directions. The greatest advance had been along the Strand towards the royal palaces at Whitehall and Westminster. It was here, at Blackfriars in the west end of the city, that Shakespeare bought a house in 1613. To the south the Thames served as a sewer and a highway for hundreds of boatmen and barges. The magnificent stone arches of London Bridge supported shops and houses as well as the road.

The city and its suburbs contained almost everything a person could want. Palaces in the west, great houses along the Strand, lawyers and their courts around the Temple. Fish were sold at Billingsgate, footwear in Shoe Lane, jewellery in Goldsmiths' row. The thoroughfares thronged with foreign sailors, merchants, water carriers, ballad sellers, peddlers and beggars.

The old London Bridge in the 17th century. Many boats were wrecked trying to shoot under the arches on the swiftly-flowing current.

## Pleasure and danger

Because land was expensive, the upper storeys of many wooden buildings overhung the street. With so much humanity crammed together, crime, fire and disease were a constant danger. The court often went into the country to escape the plague. Shortly after Shakespeare's arrival in London, the plague claimed 11,000 victims (more than 5 per cent of the capital's population) in a single year. Fifty years after his death two thirds of the old city was destroyed in the Great Fire.

Despite the dangers, London throbbed with amusements, both legal and illegal. They ranged from old-fashioned gambling to new-fangled plays. Public executions drew the largest crowds. Jugglers and musicians performed in the streets. There were countless inns, taverns and ale houses. More dubious places of entertainment were based at Southwark, on the south bank of the river. This put them beyond the control of the city authorities. It was here, amid the brothels and bear pits, that many of Shakespeare's most famous plays were first performed.

If this 17th-century picture of the Globe Theatre were accurate, there would hardly be room for the stage!

# Setting the stage

An imaginative Victorian engraving of a play being performed in an inn-yard. Women were not seen on stage in Shakespeare's time.

When Shakespeare began his career as a playwright, the idea of performing plays in specially-built 'playhouses' was new to England. The Red Lion, the first purpose-built playhouse, had been put up in the 1560s. By the late 1580s, there were three more open-air playhouses in London but none anywhere else in the country.

## Miracle and morality plays

European theatre began in ancient Greece and Rome. In early Christian times, although Classical plays were still read, they were rarely – if ever – performed. In their place simple Christian dramas developed. In England these were known as 'miracle' and 'mystery' plays, based on the life of Christ or similar religious themes. By the 15th century there were also 'morality' plays. These dramas, with characters such as Death, Strength and even God, showed people how to behave. The later ones were full of comedy. The young Shakespeare may well have seen such plays performed by locals or a troupe of travelling 'players'.

Villagers stand and watch a group of travelling players preparing to put on a mystery play. This sort of entertainment gave the young Shakespeare his first taste of the stage.

### Everyman

The most famous lines in the morality play *Everyman* are spoken by Knowledge to the leading character:

" *Everyman, I will go with thee, and be thy guide,*
*In thy most need to go by thy side.* "

## The Renaissance

English drama took huge strides forward over the course of the 16th century. There were three forces of work. One was the miracle and morality plays. The second was the Renaissance, which re-awakened interest in Classical drama. In 1562, for example, a tragedy was written in English based on the style of the Roman playwright Seneca. The third influence was Italian drama, known as *commedia dell' arte*. Italian actors brought their shows to England in the second half of the 16th century. Shakespeare almost certainly saw, and learned from, these professional performances.

The earliest known modern-style play in English was *Ralph Roister Doister*. A schoolmaster wrote it in about 1553 for his pupils to perform. By this time one-act plays known as Interludes were popular. They were put on by professional actors – the first of their kind in England - at Court and in the households of the nobility and gentlemen. In time Interlude-players added to their repertoire plays based on stories from English history. They also began performing to wider audiences in the yards of inns.

**An actor from an Italian *commedia dell' arte* troupe. These professional players had a big influence on the development of European drama.**

## Playwrights

By the last quarter of the 16th century, therefore, England had professional theatre companies. In London, as we have seen, there were also a few purpose-built playhouses. The demand for new plays was great, attracting intelligent writers such as Robert Greene (c.1558-92) and other 'University Wits' to try their hand at play-writing. They were joined by Thomas Kyd (c.1558-94) and Christopher Marlowe (1564-93). Kyd's *Spanish Tragedy* and Marlowe's *Tamburlaine the Great* (both produced about 1587) raised English drama to new heights. The stage was now set for the arrival of the greatest of them all – William Shakespeare.

### Greene-eyed jealousy

University-educated Robert Greene, clearly jealous of Shakespeare's success, wrote bitterly of the young playwright from the country:

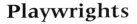 *... there is an upstart Crow, beautified with our feathers, that ... supposes he is as well able to bombast out a blank verse as the best of you; and being an absolute Jack-of-all-trades, is in his own conceit the only Shake-scene in a country.* 99

### Pick-and-mix

Although he did not go to university (very few people did in his day), Shakespeare understood Latin, French and probably Italian. He got ideas for his plays from other playwrights, from popular stories and, particularly, from the Latin writer Ovid, the Greek writer Plutarch and the Englishman Raphael Holinshed. Shakespeare's genius was in taking a story, or several stories, and changing the characters and plot to make a new play.

# Actor, playwright, businessman

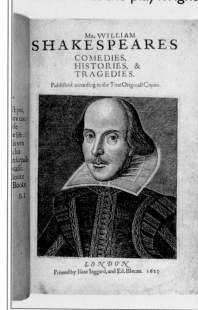

$S$hakespeare did not start writing plays the moment he arrived in London. It is said his first job was looking after the horses of playgoers outside the theatre. He certainly worked as an actor. But as we have no letters by him or to him and there were no newspapers, it is extremely difficult to discover exactly what he was doing. All we know is that by the end of 1592 he had written four plays. At least three of them, about the troubled reign of King Henry VI, drew large audiences.

**There is a story that Shakespeare's first job when he came to London was looking after gentlemen's horses outside the theatre.**

## The poet

The new playwright was noticed by the high and mighty, too. His first published work was the long poem *Venus and Adonis* (1593). It and a follow-up, *The Rape of Lucrece*, were dedicated to the Earl of Southampton. Shakespeare had time to write poetry because the theatres were closed during a serious outbreak of plague. His best-loved poems are 154 sixteen-line sonnets. Some praise an unknown young man; the others address a mysterious 'Dark Lady'.

### Full of mistakes

We have none of Shakespeare's plays in his own handwriting. Eighteen were printed during his lifetime, and 36 were collected in the famous '*First Folio*' edition of 1623, seven years after his death. Where there are two or more printings of the same play, they are rarely the same. All of the versions contain copying errors and printer's mistakes, leaving scholars to argue about what the playwright really wrote.

**Mr. WILLIAM SHAKESPEARES COMEDIES, HISTORIES, & TRAGEDIES.**
Published according to the True Originall Copies.

LONDON
Printed by Isaac Iaggard, and Ed. Blount. 1623

**Probably the best likeness we have – Shakespeare's portrait on the title page of the First Folio of his collected works.**

### *Love or like?*

Shakespeare's sonnets have caused all kinds of controversy. This extract from Sonnet 18, for example, sounds like a love poem. It is addressed to a man.

66 *Shall I compare thee to a summer's day?*
*Thou art more lovely and more temperate.*
*Rough winds do shake the darling buds of May,*
*And summer's lease hath all too short a date ...*
*But thy eternal summer shall not fade*
*Nor lose possession of that fair thou ow'st,*
*Nor shall death brag thou wander'st in his shade*
*When in eternal lines to time thou grow'st;*
*So long as men can breathe or eyes can see,*
*So long lives this, and this gives life to thee.* 99

The rewards of success – New Place, Stratford, which Shakespeare bought after working in London for about ten years.

## Wealth and fame

When the theatres re-opened, Shakespeare returned to writing plays. By 1600, after such masterpieces as *Romeo and Juliet*, *A Midsummer Night's Dream*, *Henry V* and *Julius Caesar*, he was the country's leading playwright. Several of his plays had been published and performed before the queen. There is even a story that *The Merry Wives of Windsor* was written specially for her.

Shakespeare was now a wealthy man. He made some money from writing plays but more as part-owner of the company that put them on. Clearly, he had a talent for business as well as writing. In 1597, a year after his son Hamnet died, he bought New Place, the second largest house in Stratford. Although he must have spent much of his time in London, he had not forgotten his wife and family back home.

## The final years

The playwright's success continued into the next century. He wrote the fine comedy *Twelfth Night* and a series of powerful tragedies, notably *Hamlet*, *Othello*, *King Lear* and *Macbeth*. King James was even keener on drama than Elizabeth had been and took a personal interest in Shakespeare's company. As the playwright grew wealthier still, he bought land and houses and became involved in further business deals.

From 1608 onwards his output slowed. The style of his work changed, too. His last plays, such as *The Winter's Tale* and *The Tempest*, are mysterious and magical. John Shakespeare died in 1601 and his wife seven years later. Now rich and famous, William retired to Stratford in about 1611. He wrote little more after this and died on 23 April 1616, aged exactly 52.

King James I and VI, whose patronage of Shakespeare's theatre company made it the most prestigious in London.

### The demon drink

John Ward, vicar of Stratford 1662-81, remembered this story about Shakespeare's death:

> *Shakespeare, Drayton, and Ben Jonson had a merry meeting, and it seems drank too hard, for Shakespeare died of a fever there contracted ...*

# Companies and theatres

**B**efore Shakespeare's time, putting on a play was thought a lowly, even disreputable thing to do. 'Players' were considered little better than vagabonds. They needed a patron, an aristocrat who guaranteed their good behaviour. By the mid-1590s the theatre companies were based in London and had boiled down to two, the Lord Admiral's Men and the Lord Chamberlain's Men (Shakespeare's company). The latter changed its name to the King's Men when King James took over as patron in 1603.

**The Swan Theatre, 1596, the only picture we have of the inside of a playhouse at the time of Shakespeare.**

### Royal permission

When King James took over as patron of the Lord Chamberlain's Men, in 1603 and they became the King's Men, he issued this licence:

❝ *We ... do license and authorise these our servants Lawrence Fletcher, William Shakespeare, Richard Burbage, Augustine Phillips ... and the rest of their associates freely to use and exercise the art and faculty of playing comedies, tragedies, histories, interludes, morals, pastorals, stageplays, and such others ... for the recreation of our loving subjects ...* ❞

## The sharers

The Lord Chamberlain's Men was set up by James Burbage, who built the Red Lion (1567) and the Theatre (1576) playhouses. In the late 1590s, when the lease on the Theatre site ran out, it was dismantled and reassembled south of the Thames as the Globe. A company of actors and backstage workers was

**A Victorian painting of Shakespeare and his friends. Elizabethan men loved to show off their shapely legs!**

managed by the group of men who owned it, the 'sharers'. They paid a playwright (known as a 'poet'), built or hired a theatre, collected costumes and props, and met all the expenses of putting on a play. Their most valuable possession, apart from the theatre itself, was the wardrobe of showy costumes. Many of these were wealthy people's cast-offs. The sharers divided out the profits of a successful production.

By about 1609 the King's Men had two playhouses, the indoor Blackfriars and the more famous open-air Globe. In July 1613, during a performance of Henry VIII, the Globe burned down when sparks from a cannon set fire to the thatched roof. It was rebuilt, pulled down when open-air theatres went out of fashion, and rebuilt again in the 1990s close to where it had originally stood. Today the reconstructed Globe serves as a living monument to Shakespeare and the drama of his day.

## The Globe

The Globe was a polygonal building, about 30 metres in diameter and 20 metres high. A covered stage projected from the back of the building into the central yard where the 'groundlings' stood or sat to watch the play. A better (and more expensive) view was to be had from the covered galleries that curved in a horseshoe around the yard. Two small outside entrances admitted only one at a time, to stop people sneaking in without paying.

The stage was level and bare. Above, supported on two columns, were the 'heavens'. A hut housed sound effects equipment (such as a cannon ball rolling on a board to make thunder!) and machinery for lowering gods. A trap door in the stage was known as 'hell'. At the back of the stage was a curtained area, where actors could be 'discovered', and a gallery. This either housed musicians or was used as part of the play, as in the balcony scene in *Romeo and Juliet*. Behind the stage was the 'tiring-house', where the actors made themselves ready, and storage rooms.

Inside and outside the reconstructed Globe Theatre, opened in 1997 near the site of the original building after years of planning and fund-raising.

### Do not saw the air too much...

When Hamlet, Prince of Denmark, asks actors not to over-do their performance, he is probably giving Shakespeare's own views of good and bad acting:

> *Speak the speech, I pray you, as I pronounced it to you, trippingly on the tongue; but if you mouth it, as many of your players do, I had as lief [rather] the town crier spoke my lines. Nor do not saw the air too much with your hand, thus, but use all gently ...*

## Admission prices

It cost one old penny to enter the Globe as a groundling. A lower seat under cover cost two (old) pence, and a higher seat threepence. The best seats, at the very edge of the stage, cost sixpence. The price of seats at the indoors Blackfriars theatre ranged from sixpence to a staggering half a crown (two shillings and sixpence or 30 (old) pence). This was as much as a labourer might earn in a week.

# Learning the art

Not everything Shakespeare wrote was brilliant. Many of his plays are masterpieces; but one or two are not very special. The rather ordinary *King John*, for example, is not often performed. Nor is *Titus Andronicus*, although it was popular in Shakespeare's day. Even those who admire the gruesome play admit that it is not a modern audience's idea of good entertainment – some scholars even suggest that Shakespeare wrote it as a parody of bad playwriting!

## First steps

Shakespeare took a while to learn to adapt stories to his needs. An early play, *The Comedy of Errors*, is heavily based on a play by the Latin author Plautus. Shakespeare's version is clever and complicated (it involves two sets of identical twins), and quite difficult for a modern audience to follow.

This raises the question of taste. Our likes and dislikes are not the same as those of the Elizabethans. For example, while they may have roared with laughter at the way Petrucio bullies his awkward wife in *The Taming of the Shrew*, we find such behaviour unpleasant.

### Naughty play-makers

Many of Shakespeare's early plays (such as *The Comedy of Errors*, *The Two Gentlemen of Verona*, and *Love's Labour's Lost*) were comedies. Sir Philip Sidney, the well-known courtier and writer, explained that the purpose of comedy was to show people their faults. It was not to be confused with

> *... the comic, whom naughty play-makers and stage-keepers have justly made odious. ... Only thus much now is to be said, that the comedy is an imitation of the common errors of our life, which [it] representeth in the most ridiculous and scornful sort that may be, so as it is impossible that any beholder can be content to be such a one.*

**Sir Philip Sidney (1554-86), equally at home with the pen or the sword**

## Infected air

The City of London authorities, particularly the puritans among them, did not approve of the theatre and were keen to close the playhouses whenever they could. An outbreak of the plague gave them an excellent excuse. The disease was believed to spread through 'infected air'. This made large gatherings, such as theatre audiences, dangerous. In fact, the plague was spread by fleas carried on rats and other animals.

**The Black Death strikes victims of the bubonic plague during the last major outbreak in London**

## Thy husband is thy lord

At the end of *The Taming of the Shrew*, Petruchio's wife Kate wins a bet for him by explaining how wives should obey their husbands. Modern audiences find her words hard to take and wonder whether Shakespeare meant them to be taken seriously:

> 66 *Thy husband is thy lord, thy life, thy keeper,*
> *Thy head, thy sovereign, one that cares for thee,*
> *And for thy maintenance commits his body*
> *To painful labour both by sea and land,*
> *To watch the night in storms, the day in cold,*
> *Whilst thou liest warm at home, secure and safe.* 99

## Who wrote what?

Plays were changing all the time. A playwright wrote his version, which others might add to or change. An actor was not given the whole text, but only his own part. This was to stop the play falling into the hands of another company. During rehearsal, and even during performance, the actors got their words wrong, or deliberately changed them. A complete version of the play appeared only when it was printed. In Shakespeare's case this was sometimes many years after the first performance, by when all kinds of alterations and errors had slipped in.

The hunchback Richard III, one of Shakespeare's finest creations and the most memorable of all stage villains (here played by Anthony Sher).

## More than just a story

Shakespeare had a special talent for creating unforgettable characters. One of the most famous appeared in *Richard III*, which was first put on around 1593. On the surface the play is just a continuation of the Wars of the Roses story begun in *Henry VI* – a warning to Elizabethans of what could happen if law and order broke down. What makes *Richard III* different is that Shakespeare became really interested in the main character. He did not want to make King Richard a straightforward villain. Instead, he looked into his mind and tried to explain why he was evil and what made him tick. As a result, although we hate the cruel king, we cannot help liking him, too.

# The Master

When Shakespeare's plays were first printed they were divided into comedies, tragedies and histories. These were the traditional types of play at that time. Most of the plays Shakespeare wrote while Elizabeth was queen fall into one of these categories. But some do not. *Richard II*, first performed as early as 1595, was a mix: part-history, part-tragedy.

## Comedies and tragedies

A comedy was not simply a funny play, but one that moved from confusion and chaos towards a happy ending. It was based on an encouraging view of human nature and often ended in marriage. A good example is *A Midsummer Night's Dream*, which was first put on in about 1595.

Tragedy was the opposite of comedy. It developed from a situation in which everything seemed fine to an unhappy ending (usually death). Needless to say, it gave a gloomy view of human existence. *Richard II*, which Shakespeare wrote at about the same time as *A Midsummer Night's Dream*, begins with the young king in control of his kingdom. By the end he has been deposed and murdered. Interestingly, the comedies usually have general titles, such as *Much Ado About Nothing*, while the tragedies are named after their principle characters, such as *Antony and Cleopatra*.

**Modern scholars are not so sure about dividing Shakespeare's plays into comedies, histories and tragedies, as they were in the First Folio, 1623.**

## Histories

Many of the ideas about comedies and tragedies were carried over from Greek and Roman times. Histories (or 'Chronicles'), on the other hand, were a new type of play. Shakespeare played an important part in their development. He clearly enjoyed the freedom history plays gave him. In the two parts of *Henry IV*, for example, he mixed comedy and tragedy, high life and low life.

**Sir John Falstaff examines army recruits in *Henry IV, Part II*. The greasy, dishonest but loveable knight is Shakespeare's most memorable comic character.**

History plays also gave Shakespeare an opportunity to deal with questions that concerned all Elizabethans, such as the power of monarchs and rebellion.

### When degree is shaked

In 1601 the hot-headed Earl of Essex tried to raise the city of London in rebellion. He failed and was executed. His behaviour reminded people what might happen if they tried to upset 'degree' – the natural order of things. In *Troilus and Cressida*, Ulysses told his audience:

> ... O, when degree is shaked,
> Which is the ladder of all high designs,
> The enterprise is sick. How could communities,
> Degrees in schools, and brotherhoods in cities,
> Peaceful commerce ...
> Prerogative [rights] of age, crowns, sceptres, laurels,
> But by degree stand in their place?

The talented, hot-headed Robert Devereux, Earl of Essex (1567-1601), whose rebellion soured the last years of Elizabeth's long reign.

## Two a year

Shakespeare's output was considerable. In the ten years between 1592 and 1602 he wrote about 20 plays. These included almost all his history plays, most of his great comedies (*As You Like It* and *Twelfth Night*, as well as *Much Ado About Nothing* and *A Midsummer Night's Dream*) and his early tragedies, including *Hamlet*.

His range was enormous. He could handle love as a tragic theme, as he did in the poetic *Romeo and Juliet*, or turn it to pure farce, as in *The Merry Wives of Windsor*. In short, he was the master of his art.

### The kingdom is a body

The poet Nicholas Breton set out the traditional Elizabethan view of order and government in his pamphlet *A Murmurer*. To attack the way things were, he argued, was to attack God's work:

> God made all the parts of the body for the soul
> and with the soul to serve him, and all subjects in
> a kingdom to serve their king and with their king
> to serve Him. If the head of the body ache, will
> not the heart be greatly grieved, and every part
> feel the pain of it?

### Pleasing the King

We do not know Shakespeare's own political views. Part of his genius is that his characters give their views, not those of the author. Even so, he made every effort to keep in with the court. *Macbeth*, set in Scotland, was written to please the Scottish king James I. It was short, because the new king liked short plays, and included witches because he was an expert on witchcraft.

Witchcraft was taken very seriously in Shakespeare's time, when women were still executed as witches.

# The height of tragedy

Shakespeare's plays became more serious as he got older. He also experimented with different types of play. *All's Well That Ends Well*, which he wrote around 1602, is sometimes called a 'dark comedy' or a 'problem play'. *Troilus and Cressida*, written about the same time, is even more difficult to label. Some scholars have seen it as a comedy, others as a tragedy. His last plays, as we shall see, were even more unusual.

### The uncertainty of this world

Sir Philip Sidney had no doubts about the value of tragedy,

> *that openeth the greatest wounds, and showeth forth the ulcers that are covered with tissue; that maketh kings fear to be tyrants, and tyrants manifest [show] their tyrannical humours; that with stirring the affects of admiration and commiseration teacheth the uncertainty of this world, and upon how weak foundations gilden roofs are builded.*

Jonathan Pryce as Macbeth in a 'realistic' production of the play, 1986. Actors are superstitious about using the play's name and refer to it as 'the Scottish play'.

## Rich writing

At the same time, Shakespeare's style of writing was becoming richer and more complicated. When Macbeth is about to commit his first murder, for example, he says, 'If it were done when 'tis done, then 'twere well / It were done quickly.' At first the sentence does not seem to make much sense. This is because Shakespeare has missed out unnecessary words. What he means is, 'If it [the murder] were over and done with for good when it's done, then it were just as well it is done as quickly as possible.' Shakespeare was only doing what we all do in everyday speech when we say 'See you!' instead of 'I hope to see you later.'

## Parts for the boys

At this stage in his life Shakespeare was fascinated by tragedy. We do not know why - some personal unhappiness may have depressed him. His four greatest tragedies, *Hamlet*, *Othello*, *King Lear* and *Macbeth*, appeared within five years. The parts were

written with certain actors in mind. A fellow sharer, Richard Burbage, took the leading roles. Another, Robert Armin, played the clown parts, such as the Fool in *King Lear*.

As women did not act in public, young women's parts were played by boys. Shakespeare's company must have employed very talented youngsters when he wrote the parts of Hamlet's girlfriend (Ophelia), Othello's wife (Desdemona), Lear's daughters (Goneril, Regan and Cordelia) and Lady Macbeth. The boy who played Lady Macbeth probably also played Cleopatra in *Antony and Cleopatra*. Older women, such as Hamlet's mother, may have been played by men.

**Lady Macbeth as played by Amanda Root in 1988. The part was originally taken by a boy, who must have had exceptional talent.**

## Four of the best

The four tragedies are about noble people whose lives go horribly wrong. Hamlet realises his father has been murdered but cannot bring himself to do anything about it. Othello, a great general, kills his wife out of false jealousy. The vain King Lear trusts his two wicked daughters and mistreats the honest one. Macbeth, another great general, lets his ambition get the better of him. He murders King Duncan, seizes the throne and becomes a tyrant.

All four tragic heroes die. Before they do, Shakespeare has examined their innermost thoughts and ideas. In the process he creates some of the most powerful and interesting plays ever written in any language.

### Comic relief

Shakespeare understood that an audience could have too much painful tragedy. After Macbeth has murdered King Duncan, a drunk porter comes on stage. His vulgar jokes bring much needed comic relief!

**Nowadays the part of Othello the Moor is nearly always taken by a black actor (here, Willard White).**

### *Poor player*

On hearing of the death of his wife, Macbeth loses all hope. In his despair he ironically compares human life to a poor actor playing a part in a play:

> *Life's but a walking shadow, a poor player*
> *That struts and frets his hour upon the stage,*
> *And then is heard no more. It is a tale*
> *Told by an idiot, full of sound and fury,*
> *Signifying nothing.*

# Last romance

Comedies usually ended with the good rewarded and the bad punished. But Shakespeare was so interested in outcasts and misfits (the 'villains') that he often made them more human than the virtuous people. So their punishment at the end of the play leaves us feeling uncomfortable. This is the case in *The Merchant of Venice*. We have such sympathy for the so-called villain – a Jew named Shylock – that the play is often called a tragi-comedy.

**Shakespeare's plays tackle issues that concern every generation and culture. *The Merchant of Venice*, for example, looks at racism.**

## Romances

At the end of his career Shakespeare wrote more plays with a tragi-comic feel. They have sometimes been called 'romances'. *Cymbeline*, *The Winter's Tale* and *The Tempest* are all good examples. Their plots look bleak. Then, at the very end, all turns out well after all. In *The Winter's Tale* a statue of Queen Hermione, supposedly dead for sixteen years, comes to life as the queen herself. The romances combine fact and fiction, story and reality so closely it is not easy to tell which is which. It is almost as if Shakespeare is telling us that life and the world are an illusion, like his plays.

### Pun fun

The Elizabethans loved puns, and Shakespeare gave them plenty to enjoy. In *Richard II*, for example, the dying John of Gaunt plays on his own name: 'Gaunt am I for the grave, gaunt as a grave.'

## Poetry

**The pear-shaped lute, one of the most popular musical instruments of Shakespeare's day.**

Most of Shakespeare's characters speak in verse. *Richard II* is all verse and in only three plays is there more prose than verse. (As a rule of thumb, the high-born speak verse and the low-born prose.) Verse does not necessarily mean rhyme, however. *A Midsummer Night's Dream* is unusual in that forty per cent of its verse rhymes. In *The Winter's Tale* it is only two per cent. Shakespeare uses mostly 'blank verse' - lines of poetry carried along by their rhythm but without a rhyme at the end.

The style of the poetry in the last plays is sophisticated. The sense of many lines runs on from one to the next. There is lots of music, too, and strange appearances of spirits and deities. Shakespeare may have written the plays for performance in the indoor Blackfriars theatre. Here the enclosed space and artificial light would help create a magical atmosphere. He may also have been influenced by the masque, an extravagant type of dramatic entertainment popular at court.

Prospero, the exiled Duke of Milan, whose magical powers raise the storm that begins Shakespeare's poetic late play, *The Tempest*.

# Something for everyone

As we have seen, Shakespeare was an excellent businessman. Although an intellectual, he knew his plays had to appeal to all sorts of people. Even his serious plays included dirty jokes and slapstick alongside noble thoughts and high-minded speeches. The great tragedies, however, were on the whole heavy going. Now, near the end of his life, he set aside some of this earnestness. *The Tempest*, his last great play, included songs, shipwreck, magic, love, philosophy, rolling drunks, would-be murderers, spirits - and a monster. Something, in fact, for everyone.

▼Shakespeare's monument in Stratford-upon-Avon church. The portly image is fanciful, for we don't even know that he was right-handed.

### Prospero's farewell

Prospero, the central character in *The Tempest*, has magical powers. At the end of the play, he abjures [gives up] these in a speech that some believe was Shakespeare himself saying farewell to the theatre:

> *... But this rough magic*
> *I here abjure, and when I have required*
> *Some heavenly music ...*
> *    I'll break my staff,*
> *Bury it certain fathoms in the earth,*
> *And deeper than did ever plummet sound*
> *I'll drown my book.*

### Curst be he

The inscription below is carved on Shakespeare's tomb. As he wished, his tomb has not been disturbed.

> *Good Friend for Jesus Sake Forbeare,*
> *To Digg the Dust Encloased Heare:*
> *Bleste Be Ye Man [that] Spares Thes Stones,*
> *And Curst Be He [that] Moves My Bones.*

# Living Shakespeare

Shakespeare's plays have been performed countless times to packed theatres all over the world. They have been widely translated and presented as radio dramas, films and cartoons. They have also bred other dramatic works. *Romeo and Juliet*, for example, inspired the New York musical *West Side Story*.

The very modern – and highly successful – film version of *Romeo and Juliet*, with Claire Danes and Leonardo DiCaprio

### Read the book

Ben Jonson, a playwright friend of Shakespeare's, wrote this poem about the picture ['figure'] of Shakespeare in the first printed edition of his works:

> 66 *This figure that thou here seest put,*
> *It was for gentle Shakespeare cut,*
> *Wherein the [en]graver had a strife*
> *With Nature to out-do the life.*
> *O could he but have drawn his wit*
> *As well in brass as he has hit*
> *His face, the print would then surpass*
> *All that was ever writ in brass!*
> *But since he cannot, reader, look*
> *Not on his picture, but on his book.* 99

## Enjoyment and interpretation

The plays can be enjoyed in a variety of ways. Some people are happy just to read them as poetry, others prefer film versions. However, most choose stage productions. These may be appreciated on different levels. *Othello* can be seen simply as a tragic tale about jealousy; but it can also be seen as a comment on the frailty, villainy and nobility present in all of us.

There has never been a perfect performance of any Shakespeare play, and there never will be. Different generations and cultures have presented (and interpreted) them in different ways. Around the time of the Second World War, British audiences and producers saw *Henry V* as about the heroic virtues of their nation. The king's battle speeches were taken at their face value: stirring calls to noble sacrifice and victory. (Later, the same speeches were played in the team coach of the England rugby XV as they drove to Twickenham for international matches.)

By the 1960s, the mood in the country was changing. War was no longer considered noble. In the light of this, directors of *Henry V* took a different line. They emphasised the king's coldness and ruthlessness, and played up the way his ambition rested on the blood and sweat of ordinary people who would rather have been at home in bed, not risking their lives on the battlefield.

## Kilts, battledress and cuts

Shakespeare's plays can be put on almost anywhere. Some productions use spectacular sets, revolving stages, sophisticated lights, recorded music and sound effects. Others take place in open spaces, with no scenery at all. The same goes for costumes. The original actors wore their everyday clothes, adding special costume (such as a crown, a cloak, a dress or a piece of armour) to make it easier for the audience to recognise who they were. Since then all kinds of costume have been worn. Different productions of *Macbeth*, for example, have seen actors in black jeans and T-shirts, battledress and kilts.

Styles of production change, too. Modern ones tend to be very energetic, with everyone rushing about. In the 18th and 19th centuries leading actors and actresses liked to remain quite still, particularly when delivering a famous tragic speech. Lines, even whole scenes, have been omitted. The Victorians did not approve of Elizabethan smuttiness and cut it out or changed the words.

The genius of Shakespeare is that he rises above all interpretations and translations, and speaks to us as clearly as to those who thronged into the Globe over 400 years ago.

**A Japanese production of *A Midsummer Night's Dream***

### Still with us

Many of Shakespeare's phrases crop up in modern speech. Here are just a few of the better known ones:

66 All's Well That Ends Well; *All the world's a stage* (As You Like It); *Neither a borrower, nor a lender be* (Hamlet); *To be, or not to be: that is the question* (Hamlet); *Once more into the breach, dear friends* (Henry V); *Friends, Romans, countrymen, lend me your ears* (Julius Caesar); *Nothing will come of nothing* (King Lear); *Is this a dagger which I see before me?* (Macbeth); *When shall we three meet again?* (Macbeth); *Tomorrow, and tomorrow, and tomorrow* (Macbeth); *A pound of flesh* (The Merchant of Venice); Much Ado About Nothing; *A horse! A horse! My kingdom for a horse!* (Richard III); *O Romeo, Romeo! Wherefore art thou Romeo?* (Romeo and Juliet); *If music be the food of love* (Twelfth Night). 99

| WHAT HAPPENED WHEN | | SHAKESPEARE'S WORKS |
|---|---|---|
| Wars of the Roses end | 1487 | |
| Elizabeth I becomes queen | 1558 | |
| William Shakespeare born | 1564 | |
| Mary Queen of Scots replaced by her son James VI. She flees to England the next year | 1567 | |
| William marries Anne Hathaway | 1582 | |
| Susanna Shakespeare born | 1583 | |
| Sir Walter Raleigh attempts to set up a colony (Virginia) in America | 1584 | |
| Hamnet and Judith Shakespeare (twins) born | 1585 | |
| War with Spain | 1586 | |
| Mary Queen of Scots executed | 1587 | |
| Spanish invasion attempt (Armada) defeated William comes to London about this time | 1588 | |
| | 1588-93 | The Comedy of Errors |
| | 1588-92 | Henry VI, Part I<br>Henry VI, Part II<br>Henry VI, Part III |
| | 1588-95 | Love's Labours Lost |
| | 1590-97 | King John |
| Definite evidence that William in London | 1592 | Venus and Adonis (poem) |
| Serious outbreak of plague in London. London theatres closed until 1594 | 1592-93 | Richard III |
| | 1592-94 | Titus Andronicus |
| | 1593-94 | The Rape of Lucrece (poem)<br>The Taming of the Shrew<br>The Two Gentlemen of Verona |
| | 1593-1600 | The Sonnets |
| Titus Andronicus printed | 1594 | |
| | 1594-96 | Romeo and Juliet<br>A Midsummer Night's Dream |
| | 1595 | Richard II |
| William gets a coat of arms for his family<br>Hamnet dies | 1596 | |
| | 1596-97 | The Merchant of Venice |
| William buys New Place in Stratford | 1597 | |

28

| WHAT HAPPENED WHEN | | SHAKESPEARE'S WORKS |
| --- | --- | --- |
| | 1597-98 | Henry IV, Part I |
| | 1597-1601 | Henry IV, Part II |
| | 1598-1600 | The Merry Wives of Windsor |
| | 1598-99 | Much Ado About Nothing |
| Globe Theatre built | 1599 | Henry V |
| | 1599-1600 | Julius Caesar |
| | 1600-01 | As You Like It |
| | 1600-02 | Hamlet |
| Earl of Essex's rebellion fails | 1599-1600 | Twelfth Night |
| William buys land in Stratford | 1602 | Troilus and Cressida |
| | 1601-02 | |
| Death of Elizabeth I. James VI & I becomes king | 1603 | All's Well That Ends Well |
| | 1603-04 | |
| Peace with Spain | 1604 | Othello |
| | 1604-09 | Measure for Measure |
| Roman Catholic Gunpowder Plot against the king and parliament | 1605 | Timon of Athens |
| | 1605-06 | King Lear Macbeth |
| | 1606-07 | Antony and Cleopatra |
| | 1607-09 | Coriolanus |
| | 1608 | |
| King's Men get use of Blackfriars playhouse Mary Shakespeare (mother) dies | 1608-09 | Pericles |
| Sonnets published | 1609 | |
| | 1609-10 | Cymbeline |
| | 1610-11 | The Winter's Tale |
| | 1611 | The Tempest |
| William buys a house in London | 1612 | |
| John Shakespeare dies | 1612-13 | Henry VIII |
| William probably spending most of his time in Stratford | 1613 | The Two Noble Kinsmen (written with John Fletcher) |
| William dies | 1616 | |
| Most of William's plays published in the First Folio 38 | 1623 | |

# Index

# Further reading:

Good general introductions:
*Shakespeare's World series: Theatre and Entertainment, Crime and Punishment* and *Health and Disease* by Kathy Elgin, Evans

For information about Shakespeare's works:
*Graphic Shakespeare* series by Hilary Burningham, Evans

# Websites

http://www.rsc.org.uk/learning/Learning.aspx
(The Royal Shakespeare Company. Contains information about plays and education projects.)

http://www.shakespeares-globe.org/
(The Globe Theatre. Contains background information on Elizabethan theatre, the reconstructed building and education projects.)

http://www.shakespeare.org.uk/
(The Shakespeare Birthplace Trust. Contains background information on Shakespeare, his life and times.)

http://www.elizabethan.org/
(Life in Elizabethan England)

http://www.tudorhistory.org/
(Tudor history: monarchs and daily life)

http://www.historylearningsite.co.uk/tudor_london.htm
(Tudor London)

http://shakespeare.mit.edu/
(The plays of Shakespeare)